Reflections

December 2016

Andy

I hope you enjoy
these reflections. I
wish you the best as
you reflect on your
life and ministry.

Sam

REFLECTIONS

101 Poems

By

Samuel Templeman Gladding

Samuel Templeman Gladding

library partners press

a digital publishing imprint

Produced and Distributed By:

Library Partners Press
ZSR Library
Wake Forest University
1834 Wake Forest Road
Winston-Salem, North Carolina 27106

 library partners press

a digital publishing imprint

www.librarypartnerspress.org

Manufactured in the United States of America

DEDICATION

In honor and memory of my maternal grandmother, Inez Barnes Templeman, aka, "Pal," who lived in our childhood home when I was growing up. She accepted and loved me for who I was, gave me of her wisdom, and inspired me to be more than I could have ever dreamed of otherwise.

Pal (2004)

My grandmother never complained about growing old.
She showed us her arthritic finger
    that wouldn't bend back,
    and freely admitted she could not remember names.
I guess she accepted the fact
    that the body and the mind wear out
    but life goes on..

ABOUT THE AUTHOR

I grew up in Decatur, Georgia, a suburb of Atlanta, following World War II. I was the youngest in my family with an older sister, Peggy, and an older brother, Russell. My parents were Virginians: Russell Burton Gladding and Gertrude Templeman Gladding. Both the Gladding (circa 1632) and Templeman (circa 1730) families had lived in Virginia for centuries, so there was a lot of history in our family and life was full of stories. My maternal grandmother, Inez Barnes Templeman, lived with us most of the year. The presence of my maternal grandfather, Samuel Huntington Templeman, a Baptist minister for whom I was named, was a felt but unspoken presence in my life. I thought I would grow up to be just like him.

I received degrees from Wake Forest University (B.A., history; M.A., counseling) Yale (M. A., religion), and the University of North Carolina-Greensboro (Ph.D., Health & Human Sciences). I married Claire Helena Tillson from Bridgeport, Connecticut, on May 24, 1986. We are the parents of three sons – Benjamin, Nathaniel, and Timothy – all of whom are mentioned in these poems. Claire and I have lived in Connecticut, Alabama, and North Carolina. However, we have resided on Beecher Road in Winston-Salem, North Carolina since 1990.

My first professional job was as a clinical mental health counselor in rural North Carolina but I have worked as a licensed professional counselor in the other states in which we have lived. I have also served as a first lieutenant in the United States Army Quartermaster Corps. Now I am a college professor at Wake Forest having taught in Alabama and Connecticut as well as North Carolina.

I have written about 45 books (a number of them revisions) covering most areas of counseling such as group work, family therapy, ethics, theories, and the creative arts. They have been translated into a number of different languages, for example, Russian, Indonesian, Korean, Turkish, Chinese, and Polish. However, I have also written an archival book on the history of Wake Forest University during the Hearn administration (1983-2005). In addition, I have taken Wake Forest undergraduates to work with Mother Teresa in India and graduate students to study the writings of Freud, Adler, Moreno, and Frankl in Vienna, Austria. I was a mental health responder after the 9/11 terrorist attacks in New York City and the Virginia Tech shootings. Our family has had two shelties, one of whom, Eli, is mentioned in these pages.

I have traveled domestically and overseas a great deal, for example, Singapore, China, Australia, Malaysia, Estonia, England, Ireland, Turkey, South Africa, Germany, and Argentina. I have been active in the American Counseling Association (ACA) since the early 1970s, including being a Fellow in the Association and one of its former president (2004-2005). The companion book to these poems is a text of brief vignettes published by ACA entitled *Becoming a Counselor: The Light, the Bright, and the Serious.*

ABOUT THE POEMS

After receiving a master's degree in counseling, I went to work for the Rockingham County Mental Health Center. I was optimistic, inexperienced, naïve, and somewhat isolated. The Center was located in Wentworth, North Carolina, which is a small village and at the time (i.e., 1971) was unincorporated. I did not have a lot of supervision and found myself trying to capture what was happening to both me and my clients as we worked on issues that affected and impacted their lives.

One way I found for dealing with the situations I faced was writing poetry in addition to clinical notes. The poems helped me establish boundaries and gave me perspective. Furthermore, the poems I wrote over my first five years in the Center informed me about the dynamics of counseling, mental health, and human nature. I became more aware of myself as well as others.

I self-published about 30 of the poems in 1976 under the title of *Reality Sits in a Green-Cushioned Chair*. I was too quick to go to press. I did not think everything through and although friends, family, colleagues, and the general public bought copies of the book, I did not do a reprint. However, I learned a lot. I became more aware of and attuned to the importance of the affective side of life.

Now, some 40 years later, I am publishing this collection of poems both digitally and tangibly as a record of what has gone on in my mind while working with those who have difficulties and problems in life.

Included in this collection as well are insights I have gleaned of what has transpired as I have taught college courses about mental health, been actively engaged in counseling organizations, and interacted with my family. Thus the poems in this volume are about many aspects of life from the mundane to the significant. They include my own struggles to grow as a person and a professional. Likewise, I have incorporated observations of individuals, especially interactions related to client behavior.

I do not consider any of these poems more than reflections of past recollections. Yet as a composite they trace my life as a clinician a professor, a writer, and a family man while also looking at the lives of those I have worked with psychologically. It is my hope that the uniqueness and universal aspects of these verses will resonate with you. They offer a window into distinct parts of my life but more importantly they examine common characteristics of life in general.

The poems are divided into

- those that are primarily personal,
- those that are mainly clinical, and
- those that are largely observational.

An asterisk (*) indicates poems that have previously been published in counseling journals or Wake Forest periodicals like *The Student*. The date and place of publication are indicated in Appendix B.

In closing I wish to thank those who have been especially instrumental in helping me publish this work. First, my son, Tim, did an exemplary job in editing the 161 poems I sent him initially and culling out the weaker ones. Although I know Tim does not aspire to be an editor at this point in his life, I think his future might be bright in such a career, if he ever reconsiders. My former student, Karen Wilson, who is now a Clinical Coordinator at the American School for the Deaf in West Hartford, Connecticut, was also most helpful in the editing process. She was careful and meticulous in her feedback and made the poems better yet.

In addition, I am grateful for the professional publishing guidance and direction of Bill Kane at Wake Forest University's Library Partners Press in bringing this book to life. He is truly amazing, a wise, insightful, hardworking wizard! My association with him has been fun, constructive, and pleasant.

Finally, I wish to thank my wife, Claire, for her constant support throughout this process. She is sensitive and attuned to what I do and provides me with more backing than the support cables of the Brooklyn Bridge. Her humor is delightful and feedback insightful. I know I am one of the world's most fortunate.

~Samuel T. Gladding, Fall 2016

CONTENTS

PART I, PERSONAL & FAMILY EXPERIENCES, P. 1

PART II, CLINICAL EXPERIENCES, p. 47

PART I, PERSONAL AND FAMILY EXPERIENCES

I think I have always been aware of myself both historically and contemporarily. Early in my life my parents stressed living up to the high standards of my family's past. The idea that I gleaned from them was that somehow I should make the world a better place. Initially I thought I would be a Baptist minister but I realized in divinity school that was not the right path for me. My decision to be a professional counselor was. The struggle I went through is partially captured in the poem "When First Called." Even now I realize as a result of my upbringing, I do not see a difference between the secular and the sacred. To me, everything is sacred.

The rest of the poems in this section chronologically trace my life. They include:

- believing in a future when there did not seem to be much of one ("Without Applause"),
- moving to a new part of the country ("Bittersweet"),
- wishing for greater wisdom as a young man ("In Memoriam"),
- meeting and marrying Claire ("Mid-July"),
- the coming of and raising of three children and establishing a family life (pick any of the middle poems),
- dealing with comparisons ("D. C. Morning"),
- boredom ("Possibilities"),
- the death of family ("Ruth Street"),

- the celebration of friendship ("First Thoughts"),
- beauty ("Timeless Grace"),
- the recognition of the flow of life ("Rhythms of Life" & "A Poem in Parting") and
- the fact that neither I, nor anyone else, can control what our legacy will be ("Launching").

There are other thoughts and feelings here as well ("Drumbeat") and even a potential catastrophe that turns into a comedy ("Breath"). My life, like most lives, is developmental, joyful, difficult, surprising, and complex. Most events are multidimensional.

FROM WHOM I AM DESCENDED (2006)

All those ancestors who now live in me
    through pictures, stories, and memories
Have come to life collectively
    as I walk the streets of Arlington.
Some tightly knit together and others estranged
    these men and women politely arrange
      themselves in different groups
        as I envision who they were as people
        and who they hoped to be.
In the silence of my stride
    I reflect and quietly meet
      a heritage in the colorful couples
      from whom I am descended.

ANCESTRAL THOUGHTS (1988)

*A poem about Nathaniel Templeman (1751-1778), who
with his brother James (1750-1814), joined George
Washington's army during the American Revolution.
Nathaniel died at Valley Forge. James survived the war.
Both were focused on the greater good.*

Nathaniel joined a band of rebels
    and from that colonial action
        a nation sprang and a government grew.
I, seven generations removed,
    ponder the boldness of his group
      wishing for such courage
        in my deepest interactions
          while knowing on some level at times
          his resolve is mine.

APPLES AND KITES (1996)

A reflection on security and a relationship with my father.

Out on a branch of the apple tree
(the trunk full of worm holes but solid)
I inch out to fetch a renegade kite
I chased down the hill after it escaped its string.
My father stands below
watching in anticipation
(possibly with trepidation)
Ready to catch me should I fall.
Finally, my outstretched hand
finds the thin-wood and paper-covered triangle.
I pull but the tail is caught in the thick greenery.
Down fall ripe apples on my father's head.
He fumbles to catch them but fails.
(I am not surprised - he was never good at baseball).
We laugh.
What if I had been the one to topple
from the pull to free the kite?
It wouldn't have mattered.
I would still have felt safe and supported by my dad
although maybe bruised and shaken like the fruit.

REUNION (2013)

Before we were scattered across the land
like brown leaves and broom straw
blown by November winds,
we were a nation of adolescents
a force whose heartbeat filled buildings
and inspired ideals.

Before we aged
we bloomed
and filled the world with thoughts
that have long since departed.

A POEM IN PARTING (1968)

*With apologies to William Butler Yeats, and the initial
similarity to his poem "When You Are Old."*

When you wake up one morning
    and feel you've grown old
Take this poem down from your shelf
    and slowly read its well-wrought lines
    which fade like memories of our youth.
Those were the days
    on the knolls of Reynolda
    when times were measure
    in looks not words,
Those were the moments
    we wrote in our memories
    and now, like fine parchment,
    though faded they remain
    clear impressions
    in the calmness of age,
    bringing warmth and smiles
    to the chill of the season:
brightness to a world full of grey.

WHEN FIRST CALLED (1970)

A poem written in my early 20s when trying to decide
between being a minister and being a counselor.

Templeman/Gladding travels in me
a restless presence, a history
of time and people who walked the world
long before my birth.
I feel their presence collectively
celebrate their lives individually
and listen almost reverently
for their directions
in guiding me
to what my path in life should be.
At dawn, while sleeping lightly
soft distant voices whispers:
"Eli called you 'son'
And Yahweh called you 'Samuel.'"
Awakened by the message I wonder
how to respond to a calling
from humanity and the divine
how to step forward from the mundane
and still reach out for the sublime.

These compelling thoughts and questions
make me restless in my soul
and I wrestle with the unknown
as Jacob did in times of old.
The answers are out there.
I just don't know where.
God knows.

WITHOUT APPLAUSE (1974)

A poem of hope and vision in the absence of reality.

At thirty-five, with wife and child
a Ph.D.
and hopes as bright as a full moon
on a warm August night,
He took a role as a healing man
blending it with imagination,
necessary change and common sense
to make more than an image on an eye lens
of a small figure running quickly up steps.
Quietly he traveled
like one who holds a candle to darkness
and questions its power
So that with heavy years, long walks,
shared love, and additional births
He became as a seasoned actor,
who, forgetting his lines in the silence,
stepped upstage and without prompting
lived them.

BITTERSWEET (1982)

In the cool grey dawn of early September,
I place the final suitcase into my Mustang
and silently say "good-bye"
to the quiet beauty of North Carolina.
Hesitantly, I head for the blue ocean-lined coast
of Connecticut
bound for a new position and the unknown.
Traveling with me are a sheltie named Eli
and the still fresh memories
of our last counseling session.
You, who wrestled so long with fears
that I kiddingly started calling you Jacob,
are as much a part of me as my luggage.
Moving in life is bittersweet
like giving up friends and fears.
The taste is like smooth, orange, fall persimmons,
deceptively delicious but tart.

IN MEMORIAM (1988)

I stand before the markers of my life,
like a veteran in front of the Vietnam wall in D.C.
looking at names from a long-ago war
and reliving actions in my mind.

Behind me is a younger man
a sometimes reflective stoic
who surprised by the depths of his feelings
ambivalently struggles to take charge
in a world full of turmoil without clear direction.

I watch his uncertainty with dismay
wincing in my mind as he falters,
wanting to tell him each soldier's story
of boldness or brokenness in action
and help him come to an inner peace
while giving myself relief as well.

But the insight from age is nontransferable
and his innocence lost, like the black marble,
is alive to interpretation
of events which cannot be altered.

MID-JULY (1985)

A poem for Claire on her leaving Alabama to go back to Connecticut.

I've never thought of mid-July
    as the beginning
        or the end of a season.
Somehow, it doesn't seem right
  to change directions in mid-summer.
But relationships don't know seasons.
They are immune to the tugs of the moon
      and the heat of the noonday sun.
They have a life of their own just like us.

Two seasons ago, I noticed you
    somewhere in the Monday night
        Westport crowd.
You weren't trendy, just vivacious!
That was a time when the *New York Times*
      was just a paper
      and purple only a color.
I did not know the difference between
    mauve and magic –
Then I thought I'd never care ...
    but now I do.

For over time I've come to realize
　　our relationship
　　　is more than the ups and downs
　　　　of People's Express and Delta.
It is a sharing of "Nutmeg sophistication"
　　and the "Giant Peach" on Interstate 85 –
　　　a blending of the unexpected –
　　　like tasting catfish and hushpuppies
　　when your palate has been conditioned
　　　　to the sweetness of lobster and butter.
It is the softness of a touch
　a kiss at the end of the day,
　shared panic in getting out of LaGuardia
　　and the mutual joy at the completion
　　　of another school term.
It is a smile at the gift of shoes
　　and a good joke,
　　　the relaxation of just being.

Over the past ten days we've traveled
　　more emotional miles
　　　than I ever knew existed.
I've watched you share
　　　kindness and coffee
　　　edit my writing,
　　　　charm my colleagues,
　　　　　do comparative shopping,
　　　　　make cheese omelets,
　　　　　　and give Eli, the dog, friendly pats.
Amid all the commotion
　　of a hectic schedule
　　　you've been as calm as an inland lake,
　　　and more fun than fireworks
　　　　on the Fourth of July.

Now as the minutes of your visit
      wear down
      and the engines of your plane
          warm up
I try to say "good-bye"
    in a meaningful way
    and thank you for the memory
        of your presence
              in the mid-July of my life.
The task is not as easy
        as giving you carnations and hugs
          but as you go I am ever aware
        that all my colors, words,
            and expectations have changed
                for the better in the light of you.

PRESENT VOWS AND MEMORIES (1987)

In the lighting of candles and exchanging of vows
  we are united as husband and wife.
In the holiday periods of nonstop visits
   we are linked again to our roots.
Out of crises and the mundane
  we celebrate life
    appreciating the novel
     and accepting the routine
      as we meet each other anew
        amid ancestral histories and current reflections.
Families are a weaver's dream
  with unique threads from the past
    that are intertwined with the present
      to form a colorful tapestry
        of relationships in time.

MILESTONE (1988)

My son, Benjamin, rolls over in his crib
to the applause of his mother and delight of himself
while I catch an afternoon flight to Saint Paul
to conduct a counseling seminar.
These are milestones in our lives
marking steps in our family's development
as we reach out to touch
and are changed through our behaviors.
At 33,000 feet, I drift in and out of sleep
aware that in the process, but on a different level,
my wife and child do the same.
In the construct of images and depth of thought
we attempt in special ways
to bridge the gap of distance.

NOVEMBER 13TH (1989)

After giving birth to Nathaniel
   you asked for a Wendy's shake and fries.
I can still remember, as if yesterday,
   the words that broke the silence
    surrounding the miracle of new life:
"I'm hungry."
Walking from your room still dazed
   through the Sunday streets of Birmingham
    I brought you back your first request from labor.
That cold November morning
   is now a treasure in my mind
    as are you and the child that you delivered.

AN IMAGE OF TIMOTHY (1991)

In my mind there's a picture of Timothy
  and a vision of nonverbal memories.
Awakened to that awareness
  I walk lightly and with joy --
    a man having watch the birth of his son
    and vicariously experienced the labor.
White clouds blow in the cool March air
  but my sight is focused on a previous night
  when new movement came to life
    in the rhythmic cry of an infant.

SILENT NIGHT (1994)

*Recollections of Tim Gladding as an infant
in a body cast.*

My arms still ache
   when I think of carrying you
      in your supposedly "light weight" body cast
      (that must have weighted ten pounds).
Even though it was Christmas time
    I was not of good cheer,
      despite the bright lights and joy of the season,
      except on the rare occasions
        when you quickly and quietly fell asleep
         and I could lay you gently in your crib
         for a night of peace on earth.

ELI (1993)

As an old dog, he has survived
  the marriage of his master to a Nutmeg woman,
    the first clumsy steps of sandy-haired toddlers,
      and the crises of moves around eastern states.
So in the gentle first light of morning
  he rolls leisurely in piles of yesterday's clothes
    left over from last night's baths by little boys.
Then slowly, with a slight limp,
  he enters his daily routine,
    approaching the kitchen at the breakfast rush hour
      to quietly consume spilled cereal
        and dodge congested foot traffic.
Sure of his place in a system of change
  he lays down to sleep on an air vent.
A family grows around him.

BEECHER ROAD (1993)

I walk thoughtfully down Beecher Road
   at the end of a summer of too little growth,
     the autumn wind stirring around me
      orange remnants of once green leaves.
I am the son of a fourth grade teacher
   and a man who excelled in business,
     a descendant of Virginia farmers
      and open-minded Baptists,
        the husband of a Connecticut woman,
        the father of preschoolers.
Youngest of three, I am a trinity
    counselor
     teacher
      writer.
Amid the cold, I approach home,
   midlife is full of surprises.

NATHANIEL'S ENTRANCE (1992)

He counts the coat hooks up to 39
    that line the wall from the door to his class.
An unrefined scientist, at the age of four,
    he delights in adding up objects
    that fill his world with fascination.

BOUNDARIES (1992)

As a child of five he played in leaves
 his father raked on autumn days,
  safe in the knowledge
   that the yard was home
   and that dinner
    would be served at sunset.

Now middle-aged he examines fences,
 where from within
  his own children frolic
   in the deep shadowed light of dusk,
Aware that strong boundaries
 help create bonds
  that extend time and memories
   beyond the present.

A SNAPSHOT OF TIM IN FOURTH GRADE (2000)

A Fan of Garfield, Snoopy, Calvin and Hobbes
 He names his erasers after one he called "Bob"
And further stimulates our sensations
 By using his growing imagination.

A NOTE TO TIM ON LIFE (2003)

Compared to others
   you're physically small
      so your heart must be big
       and your senses strong;
Amid such a contrast people may see
    the gifts that you bring to humanity
    and know anew that quality
      is not measured in inches.

D.C. MORNING (2004)

I was inside having a bagel and a Starbucks
      while he was outside
      having delirium tremors with a Budweiser;
"My life is together" I thought
      "It is as deep and as rich as the coffee."
While he must have believed his life was falling apart
      and that only a beer
      could save him from the shakes.
We were separated by a pane of glass
      and a world of different experiences.
I walked away saddened
      into a D.C. morning
            crisp with fall air and fresh pain.

POSSIBILITIES (2001)

This poem is a reaction to some business presentations – along with the two poems that follow [Daydreams and Values] – that I was required to attend when I was the associate provost at Wake Forest University.

At the Homestead in Virginia
    I sit as part of a captured audience
        hearing thoughts about business
        and bottom lines.
The words are bland and boring
    falling hard on table tops and ears.
I struggle to stay alert
    without drinking coffee or writing poetry.
It is impossible.

DAYDREAMS (2001)

I daydream
    tuning in and out to presenters
        who talk about macro and micro theories.
They are sincere but dull
        as they PowerPoint their charts with chatter.
Guiding principles direct them
        polite manners mask my disinterest.
I am out of my element and into fantasy
        but no one knows it but me.

VALUES (2001)

Three cloudy days
    and three Chardonnays
    have dulled my mind
      as I seek to absorb new knowledge
      in the early evening
        that is laced with facts
        and presented on slides.
I am impressed
    with the ethics that are voiced
      at the front of the room
        by a presenter who speaks
        about rights and wrongs
        that transcend time
          and impact people.
    It is amazing
      what an antidote values can be!

IN LINES THROUGH TIME (1990)

In the morning light I write of you
  as my dreams fade to memories
    in the midst of winter's chill
      and the smell of fresh-brewed coffee.
In the noonday rush I think of you
  as I log frail thoughts into a dog-eared journal
    during silence preceding the joining of friends
    for lunch and the taste of fresh insights.
At home, past dusk and after traffic,
  I read you some words from my pen,
    some from more intimate admirers.
At bedtime as I lay down
  my head dances with plans and emerging feelings
In that knowledge which is your presence
  my life becomes more open
    like a book in progress.
I live with you in lines through time.

PAUL (1992)

In memory of Paul Cleveland Bennett, son of Jack and Sharon Bennett, January 29-30, 1992.

Amid the white sterility of intensive care
  and the cries of incubated newborns
  I watch your parents struggle in the quiet realization
  that your life hangs by a thread too thin to sustain it.
Tenuously you fight to hold onto every breath
    until peacefully, in your father's arms,
      you give up in exhaustion
        and with a final release, almost like a whisper,
        air leaves your lungs forever.

Your mother has said her gentle good-byes
  only hours after your birth
    with her dreams disappearing
      as she contemplates her loss in the thought
      of going home in silence.

Life, like faith, is sometimes fragile
  best personified in newness
    and simple acts of courage.

BREATH (2004)

A choking incident at the Carter Center in Atlanta.

She asked if I could breathe
    as I tried to drink water
       and got up to leave
          with the bison bit stuck in my throat.
What an impression to make at the table!
 It showed I was fallible and less than able
        to cut my meat up into bite size pieces.
From behind he grabbed me
      and with arms around my waist
        he "stabbed me"
        right below the ribs.
The buffalo came out
      free to roam, as I am now,
        all over Georgia.

RUTH STREET (2005)

On the burial of Claire's mother, Anne, in Bridgeport, Connecticut.

We drove down Ruth Street
    on the morning of that chilly May day
       fulfilling your final request
          to go home.
You did not see your house
      or feel the joy of being there again
         in the Bridgeport bungalow
            where you raised three children
               with your craftsman husband,
And where in the last few years
      you had resided with a calico cat
         with the help of Althea;
For you had escaped the pain
      of being in a strange place
        away from family and familiarity
         through a sudden but peaceful death
           that caught those around you by surprise.

I know you would have been pleased
    with the respect displayed in this rite
    of connecting you with the past.
The black hearse slowed down and stopped
    voices full of emotion spoke
Only then did our procession move on
    to where you would find your final rest.

DEATH AND MY FATHER (1995)

Death caught my father by surprise.
He had other activities planned for that April day
   like weeding the garden
     and listening to a Braves game.
Yet startled as he was
  he had the presence of mind
    to empty his pockets
      before the ambulance came.
I am sure he did not know
    he had suffered a triple aneurysm
     (I doubt he would have cared.)
My father was accepting
   he loved plants and people, especially his family.
    He was aware of his own mortality.
In sadness
  I find relief
    (and even comfort)
      in knowing how well he lived.

MY WORDS (2009)

When my words come out
       they seldom act like refugees
       awkwardly and individually looking for a home.
Instead, they sweep forth
       collectively, with precision and in a cadence
       commanded by punctuation.
What a magnificent performance!

DRUMBEAT (1993)

In a world full of dreams
    you must listen to the beat
      of the drum
        that is your heart

TIMELESS GRACE (2010)

At 5 a.m. I ponder
    the magic of the morning and your smile.
The day will be long
    and before I am consumed
        with endless tasks,
           I focus on the cycle of time and you.
The hues of the dawn are light pastels
    but will give way to bright blue and white,
You beam forth now with radiance
    but your countenance will change
      with the afternoon light
I am helpless to transform the sunrise
    I cannot alter the look on your face
So I sit back, take in the moment,
    and rejoice in your timeless grace.

FIRST THOUGHTS:
A REFLECTION ON A PROFESSIONAL
FRIENDSHIP (1985)

*A poem for my former counseling professor Wes Hood
on his 50th birthday.*

Before I met you,
       I was aware of your presence
       somewhat the way
       a pregnant woman knows
       her unborn child
       or a youth knows an archetype
       like the hero.
It had been rumored to me
       that you had arrived
       in Winston-Salem from the West
       with graduate school baggage
       from Indiana and North Dakota.
I had been told you were a track man,
       with blond hair, smiling eyes,
       and all the warmth
       of a North Carolina summer.
Curiously, I quietly entered your class
       almost wanting to see you run
       when the name "Carl Rogers"
       was fired off.

Was the description true?
Were you the "track and fact man?"
And so the first day
        I absorbed no knowledge
        but etched a picture
        in my mind of you instead.

That important outline completed,
        I started learning
        and soon realized
        that unlike other instructors
        you weren't peddling information
        like the boys on Wendover Avenue
        selling afternoon papers,
        or running me around in circles
        like a show time stallion.
Rather, you were a scholar
        knowingly opening up doors
        for exploration
        and inviting a response.

I remember doing role plays in your class
        trying to look cool,
        while my palms sweated
        and my heart beat as fast
        as a hummingbird's wing.
You were supportive
        giving me a piece of the sun
        you brought with you that summer
        while encouraging me
        to explore the universe
        that was myself.

Other classes, other seasons came
        as quickly as the sound of laughter
        and as silently as sorrow.

With you I traveled the roads
to conventions and meetings
sharing all the light and darkness
that came to be.
I remember the days in Autumn best,
especially the time you critiqued
my class in Psychology.
On my 31st birthday you wrote me a letter
and revealed to me
who you were at that age.
I still have the yellowing notebook paper
you wrote it on
and when I wish to think of you
I search my files
until I find the tangible memory.

Somewhere in the local commutes,
long distance moves,
neatly typed letters,
finely-timed talks,
weekend retreats,
article rewrites,
soup bowl family meals,
births, car crises,
and rather mundane moments
You shared with me
the essence of your dreams,
like a miler reveals
his secret wishes on how to run a race.

I watched many of your thoughts
grow like seeds in a field,
some were harvested;
others still are forming.

I knew when I saw you last
        the memories we had shared by then
        would sustain me in your absence
        (even in the cold of Connecticut winters).
They did ...and still do.

Tonight, as summer creeps
        back into fashion
        I sit amid cool Southern breezes
        aware that the changing winds
        of life have seen you run
        through fifty years
        as if they were one hundred yards.

Yet I hear voices in the distance:
"Landmark years are new events...."

I rejoice with you in that thought
        and burn candles in my mind,
        celebrating the wonder
        of your spirit and grace
        that like an Olympic torchbearer
        inspires,
        enlightens,
        and leads to ever new beginnings.

RHYTHMS OF LIFE (2015)

Part 1 (Young Adulthood)
I glance at newspaper headlines
      as I rush to meet publication deadlines
The demands of life
      dictate my motions
      to get work done
      so I can relax, breathe deeply, and have fun.
Will that day ever come?
      I doubt it!

Part 2 (Older Adulthood)
My bones creak when I walk
      so speak loudly when you talk
      or else suggest
      we sit down to rest.
The hurriedness of yesterday
      has now quietly slipped away.
I still write and work hard
      just at a slower pace
            for I'm no longer in the race
            for recognition.

LAUNCHING (1992)

Amid the cascade of thoughts
  reflections flow and like a river
    weave a path through changing vistas
where there is room and time for growth
    and opportunities to settle.
At dusk I ponder the journey's end
  and in the spirit of transformation
    I quietly launch forth frail ideas
    into waters filled
      with hope
      and turmoil,
Conscious I may never see
  their final form
  yet knowing inside, peacefully,
    that others will keep the best
      on course.

PART II, CLINICAL EXPERIENCES

The writing of poems to accompany my clinical notes definitely helped me grow as a professional and gave me a lot of insight into myself and others. In addition, the poems kept me grounded and helped me explain what was happening in the lives of others as well as me. From a distance, counseling looks like a breeze. Why it's just listening and offering advice, right? Were that it was so simple!

People come to counseling, as these poems indicate, because they are hurting. Sometimes the pain is identifiable, such as a broken relationship, sometimes it is not and people grabble to explain why they feel so bad. Often fantasies are present in clients ("Reality Sits in a Green-Cushioned Chair") and many times there is anger ("Autumn Storm," "Tea-Kettle Song"). Wishes are almost always in clients' minds ("Scars").

Then there is the life and mind of the counselor. Those of us in the profession have desires too ("The Band-Aid Man"). We also have information our clients have yet to discover ("Of Frogs, Princes, and Lily Pond Change"). In addition, we learn aspects about ourselves in the process of helping others change ("Here and Now"). Every now and then we are surprised ("Portraits") and except in the case of emergencies we have to be patient ("Secrets," "Harbor Thoughts").

Change is a process that takes time, effort, and skill ("The Session"). It cannot be rushed ("Heartaches and Headaches").

IN THE MIDST OF THE PUZZLES (1978)

There is a quietness that comes
    in the awareness of presenting names
    and recalling places
      in the history of persons
        who come seeking help.

Confusion and direction
    are a part of the process
      where in trying to sort out tracks
      that parallel into life
        a person's past is traveled.

Counseling is a complex riddle
    where the mind's lines are joined
      with scrambling and precision
        to make sense out of nonsense,
      a tedious process
        like piecing fragments
      of a puzzle together
        until a picture is formed.

AS WE BEGIN IN THE SILENCE (1982)

The typewriter keys play sporadically
as the forms that define you in our files
are filled out to the soft, smooth sound
of music in the background.
Somehow it seems so sterile:
that a life that took thirty years to form
should be transformed in a matter of minutes
to the black-letter type of a transcript
that lies as lifeless as a sheet.
But the operation is painless
neat, clean, efficiently done with skilled hands
and the understanding
that in this world of records
your number must come out.
So I travel with you
amid the noise and background
of the various avenues you have traveled
knowing that with my chart list
I can check you off with the rapid motions
of an intake pencil or a hurry-up glance.

But I realize that deep-veined emotions
cannot be transformed to fit upon background paper
anymore than flat sheet music
can confine the mind of its composer.
Thus I lay down my forms
and begin with you the unmarked course
of quietly and patiently listening in depth
as we begin in the silence.

INDELIBLE (1984)

I find you there in my mind sometime
    even when I'm not looking.
Subconsciously you appear
    breaking into my awareness
    just when the surface of my thoughts seemed calm.
Twelve years is a long time to carry a memory picture;
    the lines blur and scenes become distorted,
    even the words change in the living process.
Yet there we are:
    sharing an ice cream, baroque thoughts,
    and the summer heat of Winston-Salem
    while from a radio in the background.
    Karen Carpenter croons a good-bye song.
"Write me a line that captures the season," you say,
    and I fumble, scribbling out awkward sentences
    while silently praying for inspiration.

Finally, gazing up amid the perspiration of my effort,
    I share my words in a trembling voice:
"Summer is everything we think of today,
    the beauty is more than the season."
Acceptingly you take in the thought
        indelibly writing it down
        as your brown eyes gaze toward the horizon.
Today, surrounded by the cold, blue sky of December
        and the hectic pace of seeing clients
        before the Christmas holidays,
Unexpectedly I smile
        as my mind travels back to that day:
            summer is again.

BRUSHSTROKES (1977)

With the grace of an artist
        etching fine India ink lines
        on rough sheets of manila paper
You present yourself before me
        almost complete – a one-man show –
        in stark, but penetrating, black and white.
I, who am clumsy with paints and colors,
        sit awed in your presence
Wondering why someone with so much skill
        would seek counseling
        from someone less than Carl Rogers.
But just as I am about to ask
        you draw my attention
        past the fine lines that decorate,
To the reality of a multicolored work
        where you live and ache
        with the memories of a marriage
        that was blurred and finally destroyed
        in the process of being formed.
All the pictures that you bring
        are a part of who you were
        but now deny:

The weathered timbered house
>   where you began painting
>   The hardwood forest where you
>   in the privacy of silence made your confessions
>   and cried,
These memories though blurred will not disappear,
>   or be erased in a moment
>   as if they were lightly lined pencil marks.
With that in mind
>   I find my awe changing to compassion,
As my thoughts descend through cover up talk
>   to the transparent man
>   beneath his own framed prints,
>   who can picture with his hands
>   a moment of painful movement
And give shape to a life
>   that though skilled and full of potential
>   is never finally developed
>   as long as the passion behind the artist's touch
>   lays waiting to be born in brushstrokes.

REALITY SITS IN A GREEN-CUSHIONED CHAIR
(1973)

In the midst of a day
    that has brought only grey skies, hard rain,
    and two cups of lukewarm coffee,
You come to me with Disney World wishes
    hoping I will change into
    a Houdini figure with Daniel Boone's style
    Prince Charming's grace and
    Abe Lincoln's wisdom
Who with magic words, a wand,
    frontier spirit, and perhaps a smile
    can cure all troubles in a flash.
But reality sits in a green-cushioned chair
    lightning has struck a nearby tree,
    yesterday ended another month
I'm uncomfortable sometimes in silence,
    and unlike fantasy figures
    I can't always be
    what you see in your mind.

AUTUMN STORM (1975)

Your words splash heavy upon my mind
    like early cold October rain
      falling on my roof at dusk.
The patterns change like an autumn storm
    from violently rumbling thundering sounds
      to clear, soft, steady streams of expression.
Through it all I look at you
    soaked in past fears and turmoil;
Then patiently I watch with you in the darkness
    for the breaking of black clouds
      that linger in your turbulent mind
And the dawning of your smile
    that comes in the light of new beginnings.

MEMORY TRACES (1977)

I listen and you tell me how
the feelings rage and toss within you.
A mother died, a child deserted,
and you, that child, have not forgotten
what it is to be alone.
I nod my head as your words continue
rich in anger from early memories,
feelings that you tap with care
after years of shaky storage.
As you drink their bitter flavor,
which you declined to taste at seven,
I wince in my mind while watching you
open your life to the dark overflow
of pain that has gown strong with age.

Active as I am in sessions
going with you to the marrow of emotions
our shared journey has an end.
Tonight, as you hesitantly leave my office
to the early darkness of winter days
and the coldness of December nights,
you do so on your own.

Yet, this season of crystallized rain
changes, if however slowly,
and our time and words together
can be a memory from which may grow
a new seed of life within you,
Not without knowledge of past years' traumas
but rather in the sobering realization
that in being heard a chance is created
to fill a time with different feelings,
and savor them in the silent hours
when you stand by yourself alone.

TEA-KETTLE SONG (1974)

I know how the pressure can build sometimes
in your own metallic tea-kettle world,
sporadically you whistle to me;
other times you explode!
Somewhere beneath that noisy facade
(in silence or stillness perhaps)
Feelings might flow with quickness and strength,
like the waters of the Dan or the Shenandoah,
but now they incessantly boil in your mind
steam filling dark shadows and choking conversation.

HERE AND NOW (1975)

I feel at times that I'm wasting my mind
   as we wade through your thoughts and emotions.
With my skills I could be in a world-renowned clinic
    with a plush, private office, soft padded chairs,
     and a sharp secretary at my command.
Instead I am here in a pink cinderblock room
    where it leaks when it rains,
     the noise seeping water-like under the door.
But in leaving, you pause for a moment
   as your voice spills out in a whisper:
"Thanks for being here when I hurt."
With those words my fantasies end
    as reality like a wellspring begins
      filling me with life-giving knowledge,
       as it cascades through my mind.
In meeting you, when you're flooded with pain,
   I discover myself.

PATCHWORK (1974)

She works in a world I have never known
    full of rainbow pills and lilac candles
        woven together with simple time-stitches
A pattern of color in a gray fabric factory
    where she spends her days
        spinning threads
           that go to Chicago by night.
Once with a little girl smile and a giggle
    she flew to Atlanta in her mind,
Opening the door to instant adventures
    far from her present fatigue,
    that was a journal we shared
        arranging her thoughts in a patchwork pattern
        until the designs and desires came together.
Silence now covers the air like a blanket
    all trips having come to an end;
Tomorrow's first shift begins at seven
    with fast sewing needles
        and loud humming noises.

In a beehive crowd, her hands with speed
will change bobbins and untangle yarn,
while with her bright imagination
she will knit herself a fantasy
where in restful villas
she will find the solitude she seeks.

IN THE STILLNESS OF SHADOWS (1981)

The glow goes out at the top of the stairs
    as darkness prevails in the silence.
The words from an old song penetrate your mind:
    "I think I'm going to be sad."
But neither the sound of the Beatles
    nor the bouncing green light on the stereo
Can issue any other ticket to ride
    but on that lonesome train called Depression.
It seems strange that the loss of one
    who filled your life with smiles and laughter
    brings only tears to your eyes in memory.
Life dreams vanish like station sounds
    softly in the stillness of shadows,
And unlike the fantasies of early years
    the thought of being awake mid-life
    and in pain is more sobering
    than the chill of winter's wind.
Yet the track is cleared after midnight
    and at dawn you again are awakened
    by the comfort of another voice.

It is the strength within
   that resides in hope, lives in faith,
   and pursues the possible in the light of day.

THE BAND-AID MAN (1975)

At times I envy the Band-Aid man
    who cleaned my cuts when I was young;
        painting me as a mercurochrome clown
            before he patched my pain with adhesive.
That was security: to know he would be around
    to fix all possible childhood hurts
        that come in growing into a man.
His job, I think, was easier than mine;
    for in counseling I cannot always see
        your past wounds, scars, and might-have-beens.
If I could, on days like today,
    I would, like the old man I remember,
        try with gentleness to address them.
For you sit beside me with tears in your eyes
    and I know how slowly words work to heal.

HARBOR THOUGHTS (1985)

Far back in his mind he harbors thoughts
   like small boats in a quiet cove
      ready to set sail any moment.
I, seated on his starboard side,
   listen for the winds of change
      ready to lift anchor with him
        and explore reality's choppy waves.
Counseling requires a special patience
   best known to sailors and navigators,
      courses are only charted for times
        when the tide is high and breezes steady.

SPINNER'S SONG (1985)

You spin your yarns with skill and grace
      separating the threads of your life
      into small and colorful categories.
Dexterously you weave the threads
      into the forms you wear
      depending on mood and weather.
Sometimes I think that Joseph's rainbow coat
      would look pale in the presence of your fabrics.
Yet as sessions go forth, you continue to spin,
      and I am awed by your verbal talent
      and sorrowed by the thought
      that I'll likely never know you.

THE GATHERING (1981)

He gathered the facts of his life around him
    like an old man collecting yellowed letters:
        written in his younger days
           but never really read or understood.
Carefully, as if words were made of fragile fragments
    that might disintegrate into dust,
He opened his mind
    to sort through events in his manhood
        and fit the pieces together as a whole.

PORTRAITS (1974)

I skip down the hall like a boy of seven
  before the last bell of school
    and the first day of summer;
      my ivy-league tie flying through the still air
        that breaks into breezes as I bobble past.
At my side, within fingertip touch,
    a first grade child with a large cowlick
      roughly traces my every step
        filling in spaces with moves of his own
          on the janitor's freshly waxed floor.
"Draw me a man"
  I stop and say
    and with no thought of crayons or paper
      he shyly approaches with open arms
        and quietly comes to take me in.

SCARS (1977)

As our sessions go on you speak of your scars
  and show me the places
    where you have been burned.
Sadly, I hear your fiery stories
  reliving through your memories and words,
    all of the tension-filled blows and events
      that have beaten and shaped your life.
"I wish I were molten steel" you say,
  "And you were a blacksmith's hammer.
Maybe then, on time's anvil,
  we could structure together
    a whole new person, with soft smooth sounds,
      inner strength and glowing warmth."

OF FROGS, PRINCES AND LILY POND CHANGES
(1976)

She went about kissing frogs
    for in her once-upon-time mind
       that's what she had learned to do.

With each kiss came expectations
    of slimy green changing to Ajax white.

With each day came realizations
    that fly-eating, quick-tongued, croaking creatures
    don't magically turn to instant princes
    from the after effects
    of a fast-smooching,
    smooth-talking
      helping beauty.

So with regret she came back
from a lively lily-pond
to the sobering stacks
of the village library
to page through the well-worn stories
and find in print what she knew in fact
that even loved frogs
sometimes stay frogs
no matter how pretty the damsel
or how high the hope.

TWILIGHT (1975)

When all my clients have left the office
   I turn off the silent overhead lights
     and watch a lingering afternoon sun
       like a patient court square artist
         slowly spreading gold-tinged hues
           across a wooden floor canvas
             and onto my cluttered desk.
That moment fills me with a sense of awe
  for quiet light and moving life.
Walking in twilight,
   I picture past sessions
     and wonder if lives I so fleetingly touched
       will dare envision their inner beauty
         painted in the colors and grace of time.

SECRETS (1990)

Out of the depth of your mind come the secrets
    rough diamond-shaped forms
        pressured in pain, cut with hope.
With inner strength
    you mine repressed memories
      and change your expression
        as hope is released.
Privately, I wish for more of your gemstones
    but the struggle is deep
      and the thoughts are too heavy
        to be quickly lightened with insight.
So with the group I patiently listen
    and silently applaud your emergence.

STILL LIFE (1975)

I watch the children line up like ducks
    all in a row, except one.
Noisily they ramble past concrete walls
    following-the-leader:
        a blond-haired woman
            in a light yellow dress
                who quietly talks through her motions.
Today is picture day in the school
    with a jolly old man who says cheese
        tossing tidbit compliments before boys and girls
        as they fix their smiles at him.
In just a flash roles are caught,
    a moment recorded, and lines form again.
Straight and precise the children walk
    all except one, who in dimly-lit halls,
        rapidly skips and zigzags along,
            defying a rule; defining himself.

JOURNEY (1990)

I am taken back by your words—
    to your history and the mystery of being human
      in an all-too-often robotic world.
I hear your pain
    and see the pictures you paint
      so cautiously and vividly.
The world you draw is a kaleidoscope
    ever changing, ever new, encircling, and fragile.
Moving past the time and through the shadows
    you look for hope beyond the groups you knew
      as a child.
I want to say: "I'm here. Trust the process."
But the artwork is your own
    so I withdraw and watch you work
      while occasionally offering you colors
        and images of the possible.

HOPE (2003)

She tells her story
   of pain and sorrow
     it is heavy
      like a day without a tomorrow;
She speaks again
   and highlights different facts
     her face is calm
      her manner relaxed;
Time has been extended
    hope has been awakened.

TURNING 50 (2005)

When she turned 50
    she took it hard
like breaking an arm
    or having a baby.
Awkward, painful, new,
    she was hesitant in her moves
      unsure of what to do.
Not knowing kept her going
    without clear direction.
I met her at the crossroads.

IMAGES (1987)

Newness begins as an image in the eye
    of what can be beyond the moment.
Quietly, visions develop in our minds
    like those that come when planting seed
    in the warmth of April soil.
Counseling children is an endless surprise
    of delight and rapid movement,
    sometimes tinged with the deep pain of sadness
    and a longing to see the future.
These are the mornings of joy and hard work
    bringing us the rhythmic dance
    of sunlight on hardwood
    and evenings of coolness and laughter.
As counselors, we enter fresh vistas
    in the rainbow magic
    and stark reality of fledgling life.
The memories of such times linger in our thoughts
    long after twilight has painted elongated shadows
    and the sound of school bells
    has faded into silence.
Grounded in hope and renewed in transition
    we structure the possible and watch people grow.

LONELY (1976)

Swinging from the parking meters
   agile as a monkey
     you make your way down
       the streets of Eden
passing startled people
    who know you from the laundromat
      and thought you were one of them.
I, too, wonder about your actions:
     this is North Carolina
   and not an enchanting tropical forest
    with long-leaved vines and branches.
Are you really so wild as you pretend
    or is Saturday just such a mundane lonely day
     that you felt in need of excitement?

HEADACHES AND HEARTACHES (1986)

When I leave the office with a headache
    I know I have done your work
        and you are without a plan.
When I go home with a heartache
     it is because I have seen you fail
        to capture your dreams in reality.
Give me heartaches any day
      for embedded in them is the pain
        that often leads to change.

THE SESSION (1999)

He follows her words
    to the end of her thoughts
        and hears the deep pain in her voice.
Empathically, he tries to respond
    structuring what he says
        through a theory
            that unfolds like a story in a book.
The session has begun!

HARMONY (1991)

The music of counseling varies in time
from the soft sob of weeping
to laughter's staccato.
Often the melody is found in the sound
of feeling in voices
and words rich in hope.
Within each session is a symphony
leading to inner harmony
and possible resolution.

TIME LINES (1983)

She was afraid to smile
    for time like a Renaissance artist
    had painted deep lines around her eyes
And she knew if she smiled
      the upturned corners of her mouth
      would help display the artist's craft:
      years past that were now only memories.
So, like a frowning Madonna,
      she pressed her lips tightly together
      unblinking, looking straight ahead
      letting minutes silently pass
      until rigidly, in her hardened style,
      she walked with slow steps from my office.

OF HIS DREAMS AND NIGHTMARES (1975)

All around the room
      I hear the hard clashing sounds
      of your loud poignant words
As they vibrate their way
      out from the depths of your inner emotions
      through the smoke-fogged air
      to my open never-filled mind
      which keeps expanding as each word enters
      and jostles about for a space of its own.
Somewhere in your childhood you say
      a door was locked
      and you, left out in the frightening dark, alone,
      had to fight gamely to gain an entry
      into the world of demanding adults
      and let your father know
      that you were more than a mere extension
      of his dreams and nightmares.
That was a terrifying, tension-filled time,
      its fleeting memory a mark
      left written on your mind – indelibly.
But that was years ago, remember?

Today, father that you've just become
    you may write in a different style
    a memo to your own small son
    who revolves in a world you have built with care,
    much like the cradle you constructed,
That as surely as the seasons come,
    with new green sprouting after winter's snow,
So you may be changed and unchained of the memory
    to speak softly in the waking hours
    in a harmonious rhythmic manner
Instead of flaring like a torch
    to burn long and bright with past-stored anger
    while shouting into the empty silence:
    "I AM!"

A COUNSELING INVOCATION (2002)

Under October skies and with a sense of awe
we gather, collectively as a family
with a mission and a purpose that transcends
the mundane pretentiousness
of a world that is somewhat chaotic,
dangerous, and unpredictable.

We are mountaineers, westerners, plains people,
easterners, southerners, and internationals
from cities, suburbs, small towns, and farms
with an identity connected to counseling
and with many ideas of who you are
and where we fit in the universe.

Thus our spiritual quest comes in multiple forms
Steeped in cultures and embracing traditions from
From Buddhist to Baptist
Moravian to Muslim
Catholic to Calvinist
Jewish to Taoist
and beyond.

Regardless of our beliefs,
unique thoughts
and the texts that we hold sacred
Let us reach out to one another
with reverence and respect
in a spirit of discovery
that leads to growth
in grace and wisdom.
As we develop professionally
make us mindful personally
that through tolerance, truth is uncovered
in openness, hope is nurtured
in civility, discourse unfolds
in humbleness, friendships form
and that knowledge, like life,
is a gift to be shared
in a world that is ever changing
like autumn skies.

GOING BEYOND PRETEND (2005)

Like the veneer on the surface of chairs
    how you appear is not who you are;
You pretend you are solid
      instead of looking at what lies beneath
        like ignoring the hole in a Christmas wreath.
I have seen such attempts before
    from actors on stage
      who blow up words by giving them air
        while posturing in the hope of gaining depth.
But your off-stage production is not serene
    of action and direction
      and your life need not be so ingrained and stiff
        like furniture awaiting inspection.

PART III, GROUP EXPERIENCES

All of us are members of groups. Sometimes they work well and sometimes they are dysfunctional. The nine poems in this section examine some of the experiences we have in groups, such as the questions we ask ("The Group Counseling Question"), our reactions to others ("Imitation"), and our feelings about being in a new group ("Beginning a Group"). These poems also look at who we are in a group ("The Me in the We") and group dynamics. The identity of a group, each group has a personality ("In Reflection"), and our own identity ("A Willow") are dealt with as well.

THE GROUP COUNSELING QUESTION (1993)

"Why am I here amid those assembled
            and what am I looking for in their presence?"
Inside I think I know the answers
        but for the moment,
            in the face of newness,
I quietly ponder the question.

IMITATION (1994)

You lead and I follow
    shadowing your behaviors
        like a school child imitates a teacher.
I am in charge of my life
  but in this group for the moment
      I focus on your words and actions.

BEGINNING A GROUP (1999)

Beginning a group is like the first day of school
    or a first kiss,
A time filled with excitement and fantasies.
Possibilities are before us
but we need courage,
   amid the emotions,
     to settle down
      and move on to action.

THE ME IN THE WE (1980)

Who am I in this Pilgrim group
   whose members differ so in perception?
Am I timid like a Miles Standish,
   with both feet on the ground
   letting others speak for me
    because the experience of failure
     is softened
      if a risk is never personally taken?
Or am I more like a John Alden
   speaking boldly for others
    in the courting of beauty
     but not seeking such for myself?
Perhaps I am more than either man
   or maybe I'm both at different times!
That's what scares me!
Plymouth wasn't settled in a day
   and what if I become unnerved
    in an afternoon of exploration?
Will all who sit here understand
    and overlook my failures?

Will I retreat when newness comes
   and string back to my past
   so my antiquity
    becomes a present reality
   and I am safe inside?
These questions haunt and taunt me
In the silence and before others,
I ponder the question anew.

ENCOUNTER (1995)

You speak to me and through your words
   I am challenged to change my perceptions
     to set aside views as if they were toys
       I've since outgrown.
I have to work hard when I give up old habits
  for like a child I'm still unsure
     what reward I'll receive in return
      and if it's worth the risk.
But in the process of meeting you
I slowly begin to build anew.

GENESIS (1993)

Knowing that most beginnings are awkward
    we wait anxiously for words or action
    to break the silence of this gathering
    and give our group its genesis.
Strangers to each other,
    and to ourselves at times,
    we slowly move into awareness
    of our own distinctiveness
    coupled with impressions
    of the options that surround us.

GROUP DYNAMICS (1989)

Emotions ricochet around the group
    fired by an act of self-disclosure
      in an atmosphere of trust.
I, struck by the process,
     watch as feelings penetrate the minds
       of involved members
         and touch off new reactions.
Change comes from many directions
    triggered by simple words.

A WILLOW (1999)

The group moves with a common motion
like a willow blown by March winds.
I am touched and swayed by its growth,
influenced by its ideas and sounds,
yet deep inside, amid the motion,
I wonder anew if I am well rooted.

IN REFLECTION (1993)

In the calmness of reflection
    we examine the depths of our lives
    and the purposes that brought us together.
I am amazed that out of silence
    and through sharing
    a whole new group has evolved.
In the process of working
    we have welded an identity
    from where we shall stand
    and likewise be moved.

PART IV, EXPERIENCES IN CALCUTTA AND IN POST-9/11 NEW YORK

Two of the most important times in my life are those I had in Calcutta, India and in post-9/11 New York City. In the first experience I worked with Wake Forest University undergraduates in the homes of Mother Teresa. In the post-911 New York environment I worked with the Red Cross as a mental health technician providing psychological first aid to individuals and families who lost loved ones in the terrorist attach of September 11, 2001. The nine poems in this section try to capture the emotions and thoughts associated with these two times from feeling overwhelmed ("First Impressions") to being pleased ("Mother Teresa") to being apprehensive ("What You Can Get in Calcutta"). They also examine human grief ("September 27") and responses to shock and grief ("The Phantom Funeral").

FIRST IMPRESSIONS (1995)

Our band wanders out into the streets of Calcutta
    hesitant, with a touch of anxiety.
As a veteran traveler I am calm
    sure within myself
    that I will be safe from the shock of the new.
At every corner and in between are
    beggars,
    butchers,
    and sellers of things.
    At every turn and in straightaways
    harsh realities come alive.
There is a dead dog next to a girl drawing pictures
    a deformed old man talking to himself
    the foul smells and sounds of taxis and rickshaws
    a horde of flies and feces on mounds of trash.
Amid the crowds, odors, and looks of desperation
I am not shocked -- just stunned (in denial)
    my senses have been overwhelmed.

STREET PEOPLE (1995)

They lay still like stones
    against buildings and walls
        covered with burlap sacks or coarse blankets.
Other people, like water,
    flow around the rocks beneath them.

WHAT YOU CAN GET IN CALCUTTA (1995)

This poem brought to you by Pepsi™.

You can get a Pepsi in Calcutta
    and most diseases ever known.
Be smart, have a Pepsi!

MOTHER TERESA (1996)

She looks just like her pictures
　　small, frail, stooped, and wrinkled.
It is good to see godliness in the flesh
　　full of life with no surprises.

THE WISH (1996)

I wished this trip upon myself
   when I said last year
      "I'd rather go than be a sponsor."
I've learned to be careful what I wish for --
   A wish can change your life.

THE POOR (1996)

When Jesus said: "You will always have the poor"
   He could have added
     "To see them in mass, visit Calcutta."
Within this bustling, polluted, disease-ridden city
   live a crowd of the world's most impoverished.
Yet the poor are more than meet the eye.
They are affluent and middle-class people
   down in spirit, apathetic to needs.
They are those within my sight
   out of touch with their own humanity.
They are my neighbors
   They are my friends
     They are me.

SEPTEMBER 27TH (2001)

She stands
    leaning on his outstretched arm
      sobbing awkwardly
Almost suspended between
    the air and his shoulder
      like a leaf being blown
        in the wind from a tree branch.

He tries to give her comfort
    offering soft words
      and patting her head.
"It's okay," he whispers
    realizing that as the words leave his mouth
      he is lying
        and that their life together has collapsed
        like the South Tower of the World Trade Center
          that killed their only son.

THE PHANTOM FUNERAL (2001)

He was dressed for a funeral
    and maybe he should have been
        but he was coming for a death certificate
        not a burial.
As we walked he sorted through his memories –
    his wife of two years, age 23,
        absorbed the first blows of flight 11
        and died instantly.
He could see her in his mind untouched
    as he dropped her off at work that day
        saying sweet nothings and expecting nothing
        let alone a catastrophe.
Now her picture on the wall
    with a rose and the words
        "I love you" placed beneath it
        was all that physically remained.

THE PICTURE (2001)

His picture stands out
    on a background of red construction paper.
"There he is" she says with pride.
Ruggedly built with a brown beard
    and long flowing dark hair,
        he portrays the vitality of American youth.
I look at him through the eyes of sorrow
    while she catches glimpses through her tears
      both of us knowing that all that remains
        is a life that was filled with promise.

PART V, OBSERVATIONS OF LIFE

This final set of poems is a mixture of observations I have had over the years from whimsy ("Jack Frost," "Anniversary") to surprise ("Salvation at Burger King") to deep pleasure ("Wedding Day"). There is some sadness in a few of these poems ("Depression," "The Fight") as well as joy in forgiveness ("Rainbow"). There is also some regret about who we are or how we act as people ("The Fight," "In Passing"). Like others, I see the world around me and cannot help think how wonderful and terrible it can be at times and how we must have a sense of humor and humility to successful traverse the challenges it presents.

RAINBOW (1997)

With age she has learned
    to forgive the groups
       that mistreated her
         because of her color.
Each Saturday she now bakes bread
    and takes it to the local mission
       where she stays to cut and serve it
        with love and a main dish.
Her grace has conquered years of hatred
     angry words and hours of sadness,
Her brightness exudes a subtle warmth
     everyone calls her "Rainbow."

THE DREAM (2003)

He struggles
   as he rides
      beneath the boroughs of New York City
     afraid he may have lost the dreams
       he nurtured in the open fields
         outside of Lincoln, Nebraska.
He looks for new horizons
   peeking over a sea of brownstones.

SALVATION AT BURGER KING (2002)

He found Jesus at Burger King
    in between bites and verses in Matthew.
Salvation came with fries that day
    along with a large Coca-Cola.

TIME AND MOTION (2007)

They wait
    stiff and still in the summer heat
      for the boys who loved them
        to return.
But those boys,
     now grown to an age
     where swings
       are just a part of their history
Sit on their front porch steps
    trading stories in the long afternoon
      when the girls they knew,
       now women,
         will walk by, sometimes stop,
           and send their hearts into orbit.

WEDDING DAY (1991)

He was as nervous as a cat
  in a room full of rockers
    stiffly dressed in formal black
      uptight, and afraid of moving quickly
        lest he break a button
          or the mood from the organ music.
She was serene
  as if living a dream from childhood
    dressed in layers of white
      with a lilac bouquet
        unable to conceal her contentment
          she remained poised amid the quiet
         of assembled excitement.
Together they exchanged
  formal wedding vows,
    homemade bands,
      and brief, expectant glances.
Then numbered, as if by Novocain,
  they slowly greeted guests
    and themselves anew
as they whispered good-bye to innocence
  and hello to the opening of a marriage.

ANNIVERSARY (2012)

He took her out for their anniversary
 running her down to the ground accidentally
  as he backed out of the driveway.
"Ooops" he said.
"The marriage is dead."

DEPRESSION (1978)

It comes in slowly, a whisper
    aching into the marrow of the bone
        like the chill of a dull gray winter.
Quietly it rests
    heavy on the heart in motion;
        a subtle pressure
            throwing the rhythmic beat
                ever so slightly
                    off.
Depression rules in silence
    unseen but deeply felt.

SMALL CHANGE (1996)

He changed,
   giving her small compliments at breakfast,
     such as
   "I like the way your hair looks"
     or
   "Nice dress."
She wondered,
   "What's he doing?"
     but also she knew she liked his words.
So as the days continued
   she responded to his acts of kindness
     with new behaviors of her own.
He changed;
   She changed;
     They changed.
And it was for the better!

MONDAY NIGHTS (1991)

She flips through a magazine on the blue-striped couch
    sometimes entertained but often bored,
    while he gulps down popcorn and televised football,
    feeling occasionally excited yet often empty.

At midnight when the lights go off
    the news of the day is finished
    and the games are decided,
    she lays in anticipation, but without hope,
    of his touch
    while he tackles quarterbacks in his sleep
    and ignores inner needs.

Alone, together, they form a couple,
    together, alone, they long for a relationship.

THE FIGHT (1991)

They trade insults and accusations like children
  afraid to be vulnerable and scared not to be.
Underneath all of the words and bravado
  is a backlog of bitter emotion
    dormant so long that like dry kindling
      it burst into flames when sparked.
Through the dark and heated fights
    points are made that leave a mark.

In the early morning, she cries silently
  into black coffee grown cold with age
    while he sits behind a mahogany desk
    alone.

IN PASSING (1970)

An old black man in downtown Atlanta
  is clubfooted, blind, and bends like the willows.
He sits by his papers near Peachtree Street
  passing the time by tapping his crutches.
I flow by him in the five o'clock stream
    of white-collared, blue suited, turbulent people
      rushing for trains to neighboring suburbs
        and the prospects of quiet in the flood-tide of life.
Spring rains now enrich the earth
  but where do the willows and waters meet?

JACK FROST (1969)

Jack Frost went walking last night
  and as he made his rounds
    he stopped and breathed upon the green
    fading it to a golden brown.
Shame on you, Ole Jack!
  Autumn hasn't begun
    so please breathe lighter from now on
    or better yet, don't come!!

EPILOGUE

I hope you have enjoyed your trip through this poetry. I would not have imagined I would be filling a book with poetry when I was younger. In fact, I find it hard to believe now that I am older. However, I have learned a good deal from writing and my wish is that you have "take aways" (different thoughts and feelings) from having read this volume. I have written other verse besides what is contained here. Some of it may see the black and white of print but regardless, it has served a purpose in letting me express what I needed to let go of or examine. I think writing does that for us and frees us to move on in our lives productively.

In Appendix A I have listed the chronological dates these poems were written. You will notice that many of the clinical poems were written during a time when I was very involved on a daily basis with counseling. However, some of the poems were written later like some of the poems in other sections.

Thought and feeling are like that in that they may take months or years to simmer before they emerge in an understandable form. Regardless, jotting down this information has been helpful for me in deciphering where my mind has been. It may well help you understand your own thought process. The important thing is that we get insight from our experiences and do not go through life oblivious to our inner lives or outside events.

APPENDIX A:

CHRONOLOGICAL DATES OF THE POEMS

YEAR	POEM
1968	A Poem in Parting
1969	Jack Frost
1970	When First Called
1970	In Passing
1973	Reality Sits in a Green Cushioned Chair
1974	Tea-Kettle Song
1974	Patchwork
1974	Portraits
1974	Without Applause
1975	Autumn Storm
1975	Here and Now
1975	The Band-Aid Man
1975	Twilight
1975	Still Life
1975	Of His Dreams and Nightmares
1976	Of Frogs, Princes and Lily Pond Changes
1976	Lonely

2001	Possibilities
2001	Daydream
2001	Values
2001	September 27th
2001	The Phantom Funeral
2001	The Picture
2002	A Counseling Invocation
2002	Salvation at Burger King
2003	A Note to Tim on Life
2003	The Dream
2003	Different
2003	Hope
2004	Breath
2004	Pal
2004	D. C. Morning
2005	Ruth Street
2005	Turning 50
2005	Going Beyond Pretend
2006	From Whom I am Descended
2007	Time and Motion

APPENDIX B:
PERIODICALS SOME OF THESE POEMS HAVE APPEARED IN PREVIOUSLY

Gladding, S. T. (1992). In Memoriam. *Journal of Humanistic Education and Development, 29*, 128.

Gladding, S. T. (1990). Secrets. *Journal of Humanistic Education and Development, 28*, 141.

Gladding, S. T. (1990). Journey. *Journal of Humanistic Education and Development, 28*, 142.

Gladding, S. T. (1989). First Thoughts: A Reflection On a Professional Friendship. *Journal of Humanistic Education and Development, 27*, 190-191.

Gladding, S. T. (1989). Encounter group beginnings. *Journal of Humanistic Education and Development, 27*, 133.

Gladding, S. T. (1987). Images. *Journal of Humanistic Education and Development, 26*, 48.

Gladding, S. T. (1985). Harbor thoughts. *Journal of Humanistic Education and Development, 24*, 68.

Gladding, S. T. (1985). Spinner's song. *The School Counselor, 32*, 395.

Gladding, S. T. (1984). Genesis. *Journal of Humanistic Education and Development, 22,* 178-179.

Gladding, S. T. (1984). Indelible. *Personnel and Guidance Journal, 62 (5),* 307.

Gladding, S. T. (1982). As we begin in the silence. *Personnel and Guidance Journal, 60 (9),* 573.

Gladding, S. T. (1979). A restless presence: Group process as a pilgrimage. *The School Counselor, 27,* 126-127.

Gladding, S. T. (1978). In the midst of the puzzles and counseling journey. *Personnel and Guidance Journal, 57 (3),* 148.

Gladding, S. T. (1978). Shadows. *The School Counselor, 25 (5),* 326.

Gladding, S. T. (1978). Depression. *The School Counselor, 26 (1),* 45.

Gladding, S. T. (1977). Scars. *Personnel and Guidance Journal, 56 (4),* 246.

Gladding, S. T. (1975). The bandaid man. *Personnel and Guidance Journal, 53 (7),* 520.

Gladding, S. T. (1975). Here and now. *Personnel and Guidance Journal, 53 (10),* 746.

Gladding, S. T. (1975). Of his dreams and nightmares. *Personnel and Guidance Journal, 54 (2)*, 88.

Gladding, S. T. (1975). Autumn storm. *Personnel and Guidance Journal, 54 (3)*, 149.

Gladding, S. T. (1975). Twilight. *Personnel and Guidance Journal, 54 (4)*, 230.

Gladding, S. T. (1974). Tea-Kettle song. *The School Counselor, 21 (3)*, 209.

Gladding, S. T. (1974). Without applause. *Personnel and Guidance Journal, 52 (9)*, 586.

Gladding, S. T. (1974). Patchwork. *Personnel and Guidance Journal, 53 (1)*, 39.

Gladding, S. T. (1974). Portraits. *Personnel and Guidance Journal, 53 (2)*, 110.

Gladding, S. T. (1973). Reality sits in a green-cushioned chair. *Personnel and Guidance Journal, 52 (4)*, 222.

Gladding, S. T. (1968). In passing. *The Student Magazine*. Wake Forest University.